Broken

Stained

Redeemed

by
Karen Warner Heidrick

Published by Skinny Brown Dog Media
www.SkinnyBrownDogMedia.com

Developmental Editing and Cover Design: Eric G Reid
www.SuccessLifeU.com

ISBN 978-1-7370393-1-0

New International Version (NIV) is the source file for all Bible quotes, unless otherwise noted.

The events shared in this book are based on the accounts of the author and supported by the individuals included in those events.

If you would like to contact Karen Warner Heidrick directly, you may do so at
http://www.KWHeidrick.com

Dedication

With a humble and grateful heart, this book is
Dedicated to my Heavenly Father God for His patience
and unconditional love

Contents

Foreword

Every once in a while, a person comes along who doesn't follow the rules. They play outside the box, color outside the lines, not in defiance or disdain for the rules, but simply because they don't even know the rules exist.

Karen Warner Heidrick is one of those unintentional rule-breakers. I met Karen Warner Heidrick as a coworker at the Youth Advocate Program in Newark, New York. Karen and I shared a passion for helping kids who were at risk of being involved in the criminal justice system.

What I found special about Karen was the way God was using her to heal others. There are some in the body of Christ that have the gift of healing. Some have even tried to turn the gift of healing into an income stream. But Karen was often more surprised by the healings she was called to witness than those who were healed. She was surprised because she had expressed that she did not have a personal relationship with God.

When Karen returned from her first mission trip, bubbling with excitement about how people were being healed before her eyes. Karen explained that she did not

1

even know how to pray for healing all she did was lay her hands on people and say, "Thank you, Jesus!" over and over.

God seemed to be using the gift of healing to bring Karen to a deep and saving faith in the Lord Jesus. Receiving the gift of healing and then establishing a relationship with Christ is the opposite order of how those two things usually happen. What I find refreshing about Karen's gift is that she had not read about healing, taken courses or classes to learn about it, or even prayed for the gift. It was truly a gift in the biblical sense of the word.

If you have struggled with your faith or believing that the God of the Bible still heals, or if you question whether God still uses His chosen ones to bring about miracles of healing, *Broken Stained Redeemed* is the book for you. If you are a born again, Spirit filled believer that desires a deeper understanding of the gift of healing or just want to see Jesus glorified this book is also for you. Karen's book lets us know God is still on His throne and answers our prayers.

God used Karen to heal his people not only in Latin America but in her home church. Her gift of healing become real for me personally one Sunday after church.

Karen asked me if I could come to the prayer room and pray with her for someone who needed healing. Walking into the prayer room, I asked, "Who are we praying for?" and everyone shouted, "YOU!" We had decided to pray for my healing from bipolar disorder. I must admit I was the biggest skeptic in the room in that moment.

I reluctantly sat down as *la dama con los manos calientes* as they call her in Latin America "the lady with hot hands" put her hands on my head. Shortly after Karen placed her hands on my head, I could feel the heat and vibrations that I had heard others describe. Since that day, for the last four-and-a-half years, I have been bipolar-medication free. Today, I can function more productively.

Broken Stained Redeemed will take you on an adventure of healing from the perspective of someone with childlike faith. Karen's story shows how she delights in seeing God move in people's lives.

Bob Ludwig , Ordained Minister
Volunteer at the New York State Correctional Facilities
Worship Leader, Love Fellowship Worship Center, Rochester, New York.

1

Our God is Greater
The First Miracle

It was the summer of 2015, and finally, after months of preparing for a mission trip that had once been just a dream, I was walking towards the terminal for my first international flight and my first mission trip. As I listened to the overhead announcers calling out the different destination cities, I could barely contain my excitement. I had so many questions about what lay ahead for me and how I would serve alongside the other mission team members. Standing in line at the check-in among my fellow missionaries from Cross Creek Church, I realized that that day was a day of so many firsts.

Before arriving at Miami Airport for our departure, our mission team had spent months fundraising, attending meetings with team leaders, practicing skits, and preparing our hearts and minds for serving in underdeveloped neighborhoods in the Dominican Republic. Our leaders for this mission were incredibly organized and supportive of our mission team. They seemed even more excited than we were for this trip. Many of the leaders for this trip were already serving our congregation as pastors and leading youth groups and other ministries in an already busy and growing church. Part of each team leader's job was to ensure that everyone completed the requirements for preparing for our trip, so would meet in small groups and give us heartfelt words of encouragement. During the days leading up to leaving my home in New York and heading south, I was delighted for the opportunity to visit and serve in another country for the very first time at age fifty-four. I was preparing for my first international trip and my first mission trip surrounded by many people half my age. What was I thinking? *Why not?*

During our last pre-departure meeting at the church, one of our youth pastors, Jason, shared a timely message: the bigger the mission, the bigger its challenges. He reminded us that, it included churches from around the world because of this mission's enormity, and the enemy would not be pleased with what we were about to do. An unhappy enemy will do whatever it takes to stop you from doing what you are called to do. Pastor Jason forewarned us that, at some point, we might find ourselves feeling weary, distracted, or overwhelmed, and that in those moments, we should ask God to come alongside us and keep pressing on because God is greater than the enemy. When Pastor Jason told us this, I nodded in agreement, but in my heart, I had doubts.

You see, at the time, I believed in God, although I did not have a relationship with Him the way other people talked about having a relationship with God. Instead, I saw God similar to how I saw the moon: very real, but very far away. I knew the moon was there, but I had never experienced the moon up close. I knew the moon acted on the things around me, but somehow, I felt just outside its effects. For years, I had personal issues that created a barrier between God and me. Growing up, my father was not able to be a part of my life. I still loved this stranger and all the beautiful attributes I heard about him mostly from my mother, who wanted me to be proud of him. These stories about my father, a gifted man, made me want to spend time with him even more.

It was from that estranged relationship with my father that I based my relationship with God. I learned I could find safety and comfort in loving people despite them not being near to me. I accepted that people did not need to show up in life for me to hold them in a special place a place that was filled with hope. I hoped that if I loved hard enough, those people would somehow become real. Throughout my life, I envisioned that God sat in that distant place along with my father. Sitting through church services, hearing the gospel, and attending Sunday school was an integral part of my childhood, and I embraced everything I was taught about God as truth; yet I kept Him at a distance, because I did not feel worthy of his love. After all, there had to be something wrong with me if my father had left me despite all my love for him.

As I waited in line at the airport, the team leaders reminded us to have all our documents ready in hand, as we did not want to fall behind schedule. As I opened my backpack to retrieve my passport, my heart raced with excitement for just a few minutes, I would have my boarding pass and be on my way to the Dominican Republic. As I searched through my backpack, I did not see my passport. Placing my backpack on the ground, I assumed my passport was hidden under other stuff in there, so I began frantically taking items out and setting them on the floor beside my backpack. I still could not find my passport. I recalled seeing the lime-green passport case in my backpack as I had sat in the hotel lobby waiting to board the bus for the airport. As I continued searching, I began letting others with their passports in hand go ahead of me. Since it was a bright, lime-green case, I figured I would eventually find it if I just kept searching. My passport missing did not make any sense. I had held tightly onto my backpack the entire time since taking inventory of the contents and had double-checked to make sure my backpack was securely closed.

When I looked up, I realized I was now the last traveler in line from our group. I was growing very anxious as I continued to search through my backpack; at the same time, I was keenly aware that Pastor Jason was a few feet to the right of me, speaking to a gentleman he knew from a past trip. At this point, it became evident to anyone watching that something was wrong. I kept my head down, still searching for my passport while trying not to cry. Family and friends who know me well will tell you that I tend to be overly sensitive and hardest on myself when situations are not going well. I did not want to make eye contact with Pastor Jason, as troubling thoughts ran through my mind. *Now I am not going to be able to go on my dream trip! How could I let down all of my generous sponsors?* I was especially worried about how our leaders would feel after they had selflessly devoted so much time and energy to ensure a successful and safe trip. Then I thought about having to call my sister and brother-in-law, who lived a couple of hours away, to come pick me up and bring me back to their house. As my anxiety continued to increase, and I continued to frantically search for my passport, all I could think to myself was, *Why is this happening to me?*

Lost in my thoughts and tears, I did not realize Pastor Jason had noticed my distress and walked towards me. Standing over me as I gathered up the contents of my backpack, he asked me if everything was okay. Terrified and trying to fight back the last of my tears, I slowly looked up at him and said, "I cannot find my passport!" As Jason spoke to me while holding eye contact, he asked me in a very calm voice, "Where did you see it last?" I told him I had last seen it at the bottom of my backpack at the hotel just before leaving for the airport. I also told him that I had not taken it out since then and made sure I closed my backpack securely. It was then that the gentleman Jason had been talking with asked us for the name of the hotel and the name on my passport. As Jason was giving the man the information, he appeared to search the contacts on his phone. I heard him sharing my dilemma over the phone with what I could only assume was someone he knew at the hotel. As the man walked back towards us, I heard him say, "Thank you" before hanging up. As I held my breath, hoping that somehow, I might just still make the trip, he told us that the person who answered the phone happened to be holding my passport in his hand and was on his way to the airport to deliver it to us. My passport should be back in my hands in five minutes.

As I took a deep breath, my eyes filled with tears again but this time they were tears of joy as I tried to compose myself and thanked the gentleman. I was so thankful for Jason's tremendous faith and incredible patience, especially since we were now late for boarding the plane. Jason and I said goodbye to this earthly angel, and finally, with Jason by my side and my passport in hand, I went through the check-in process and took off running for the plane where the rest of our group was waiting for us. As I processed all that had just happened regarding my passport, I reflected on Jason's last message before our trip, about the enemy working against us and the big things we were about to do. I asked Jason if what had just happened was what he had meant about the enemy hating what we were about to do and wanting to use all his might to stop us. Jason confidently smiled and answered, "Yes!"

As I sat on the plane waiting for it to take off, I recalled the scripture that talks about how the enemy comes to kill, steal and destroy. That had just become real in my life. Had God come alongside me and defeated the enemy? Was I about to do big things that needed to be stopped? We had not even left Miami, and already this mission trip was changing me.

I will always be grateful for Jason's calm nature and genuine concern for me in those moments. He truly believed that "faith can move mountains." I considered myself to be a lukewarm Christian at the time. Jason and his friend, on the other hand, had tremendous faith, which they put into action to get back my missing passport and ultimately save my trip.

Divine intervention was at work, and making this flight was the first of many miracles to reveal themselves on this excursion. As I heard the plane engines roar, propelling us down the runway, never in my wildest dreams would I have guessed why the enemy had tried to prevent me from going on this mission trip. God had plans to use me to bless others in ways I could never have imagined.

"Heal me, Lord, and I will be healed; save me, and I will be saved, for you are the one I praise."
Jeremiah 17:14

2

La Mejor Republica Dominicana
The Best Dominican Republic

As soon as I had sat down on the plane, I felt as though I had been holding my breath the entire day. Fastening my seatbelt, I finally exhaled all the anxiety I had been harboring. As I focused on inhaling a sense of peace, the realization dawned on me that this mission trip was becoming my reality. Looking out my window, I began daydreaming about what the trip would be like. I could not wait to love the people of the Dominican Republic. I had been told that our hosts were equally excited to meet us.

Sitting 40,000 feet in the air crossing oceans, I was confused about how a country that is so well known for beautiful honeymoon vacations is also home to many impoverished neighborhoods and hurting citizens. I was

13

looking forward to meeting the Dominican Republic people, who are very cordial and welcoming to visitors abroad. I especially could not wait to love the children, many of whom are orphaned. Teaching and being with children have always been some of my greatest passions and joys. Before leaving for the mission trip, I taught preschool-aged children and felt so blessed to have a career working with a population I dearly loved. My family and friends who know my heart jokingly warned me that I could not bring children home with me from this trip. In preparing for the trip, I had learned some interesting facts: The Dominican Republic is the only country with a picture of a Bible on its flag, and most people in the Dominican Republic were of the Christian faith.

On this mission, our group would join over two thousand other missionaries from all over the world. Together we would join in sharing the love of Jesus while offering hope and purpose to every citizen in the country. This would be the largest single mission group in the country's history, welcomed by the government, and several local churches and volunteers would host Our goal for this coming week was to work to bring aid to the

14

Dominican Republic and share the gospel with its citizens. Thousands of local pastors and business leaders had participated in training events held in two of the country's largest cities to prepare logistically for the week ahead. This mission would be carried out in twenty different cities across the country. Every group of missionaries was assigned various projects to improve the lives of the people who lived in the Dominican Republic. Our church group was responsible for setting up a medical clinic with medical missionaries, distributing five hundred pairs of shoes to youth, sharing the gospel, and praying with people in neighborhoods and sports fields. Most Dominicans did not have access to medical care, and shoes were vital, because they were required to be worn at school and at church services. Without something as simple as a pair of shoes, some children could not get an education. Other groups planned to build homes and churches, others would help dig water wells, and still others worked on health and nutrition programs. Having a community-owned water well was necessary because many people without a well had to buy containers of water off trucks. Buying water was expensive, and the giant jugs of water needed for a family were very difficult to transport.

As my plane touched down, I retrieved my luggage with the rest of my group, and we boarded a bus for Puerta Plata. Puerta Plata was the city we would be working in and around for the next week. As our bus full of excited missionaries entered the town, I saw dozens of people cheering and waving flags to celebrate our arrival. It was like they were celebrating the appearance of a winning sports team or group of celebrities! Puerta Plata's people were in the streets cheering and performing beautiful dances with fantastic costumes. It was overwhelming to receive such an open and welcoming greeting from strangers. Everyone along the roadside appeared so warm and friendly, just as I was told they would be. After I got off the bus, I wanted to thank all of the people for being there for our arrival, so I began walking along the street, shaking hands, and giving hugs and high fives. I soon found myself walking up to a mother who was holding a baby girl. As I approached the woman, the baby reached her arms for me, and with her mother's permission, I held this precious child. My heart leaped into my throat. I had been traveling for days and preparing for months for a moment like this, and it was happening, right here in the streets of Puerta Plata. The baby girl was smiling right at me as if she knew the rest of the team and I were there to help make her life better and wanted to offer a big thank you! I knew, as I held her amid the music and dancing, that this was one of those moments I will never forget.

After the stunning performance, we boarded the bus again and drove through some of the neighboring villages where we would be ministering to the locals. I saw so many beautiful people and marveled at how happy they were to see us despite the poverty around them. There were rows and rows of adults and children cheering and waving to us as we arrived. In my heart, I knew I was meant to be there. I did not know what I would do, but I knew that I was there for a purpose, and I could not wait to get started. Before getting off the bus for the final time, Jason and Rebecca, who also worked with youth in our church, stood up in the front and said they had an announcement to make before we exited. Jason said that our first day of the mission would include me serving in the medical clinic. Jason said God had laid it on both his and Rebecca's hearts separately that I was to serve in the

17

medical clinic. Initially, I did not know how I should feel about this revelation, and wondered how I would serve in the clinic, but I agreed to just go with the flow. After my passport situation at the airport earlier that day, I slowly allowed myself to see God's hand on this mission trip and trust that He was in control.

"And we know that in all things God works for the good of those who love Him, who have been called according to his purpose."
Romans 8:28

3

The Medical Clinic
"No More Pain"

As my three other roommates and I settled into the room where we would stay for the week, I took a minute to catch my breath and reflect on all that had happened that day. The trip had been fantastic so far, including the unexpected events at the airport in Florida and the enthusiastic welcome that had overwhelmed us upon our arrival in Puerta Plata. Wondering what tomorrow would be like serving in the medical clinic, I was filled with excitement and a bit of fear. I thought about how incredibly blessed I was for the opportunity to serve these beautiful people by simply loving on them and doing whatever I could to make their lives better.

The following morning, I reported to the medical clinic. The clinic consisted of a large white tent with chairs lined up along one side and tables near the front where people would be assessed and treated by experienced medical volunteers. Shortly after arriving and getting signed in with the team, Linda, introduced me to the man who would be serving alongside me. Linda was not only a very compassionate, supportive leader in our group, she was also married to Pastor Dave. Linda was the type of person that loved everyone she met and made them feel welcome. Linda had the gift of exhortation, and her ability to encourage and inspire others was beautiful to witness. If Linda knew someone was experiencing a difficult time, she would likely mail them an encouraging card or note.

For that day, my mission partner in the clinic would be Darrin, a gentleman from Australia. Having no medical training and unsure what my role for the day would be, I approached Linda and asked her what we should be doing. Linda told us to pray over people as they came and ask them if they were saved and had a home church. Darrin and I were also given pieces of paper to keep a tally of who needed salvation and a church to attend. Darrin and I had a few minutes to get acquainted as the people began to file in and take their seats along the wall. We were also teamed up with an interpreter, which allowed us to ask each person why they were there and allowed them to understand our prayers. Praying out loud in front of others was out of my comfort zone. I shyly asked Darrin if he would mind praying out loud first. I was relieved when he agreed.

As I watched a woman slowly making her way to the first chair, I noticed that her knees were slightly bent, and she appeared to have difficulty walking. Through our interpreter, she told us that she had a lot of pain in both knees, making it a burden to walk. The older woman also shared that Jesus was her Savior, and she attended church regularly. Looking back to that day, I recall meeting only one man who was on the fence about salvation. Darrin prayed the prayer of salvation with that man, and he accepted Jesus into his heart and asked Jesus to be his Savior. As Darrin prepared to pray over this woman, I felt led, with her permission, to place my hands over her knees. Within moments of Darrin beginning to pray, I felt the heat and then a wave-like movement between my hands and her knees.

As the heat flowed from my hands to her knees, I started thanking Jesus. When the heat and waves stopped,

I stood up. Our interpreter then asked the older woman how she felt. I was still trying to understand what I had just felt. As the woman stood straight up, she raised her hands towards the sky and said, "No mas dolor!" (No more pain!). The older woman also said that she had felt heat coming from my hands. She did not say anything about the movement of waves that I had felt. Amazed at what had just occurred and overcome with joy, together we all praised God and embraced. As I raised my arms in praise, I could feel my heart opening as love and unbridled joy poured in. It was at this moment that I believe the Holy Spirit touched me. It seemed the Holy Spirit had not only touched me but was filling the room around me. As a little girl, I had been taught that the Holy Spirit's role is to instill Christ-like characteristics in the followers of Christ. It was by the Holy Spirit that Christ had received his spiritual gifts. It is by gifts of the Holy Spirit that God empowers all of His people for ministry.

By now, every chair in the clinic was filled with people waiting patiently for medical help. As much as I wanted to spend more time with the elderly lady and explore what had just occurred, I knew I had to keep moving. Seated in the second chair was a woman who shared with Darrin, me, and the interpreter that she had pain in her stomach. With her permission, I placed my left hand over her stomach area. Now it was my turn to pray out loud. After listening to Darrin's heartfelt prayer, I was even more self-conscious about praying in front of people, but I proceeded. I began by asking Jesus to bless this woman by taking her pain away. As I prayed, I began to feel the same sensation of heat and then waves under my hand as I touched the woman's stomach. After saying a few more prayerful words, I retreated to simply repeating, "Thank you, Jesus" until I felt the heat and the waves of energy cease. As soon as the woman told the interpreter that there was no more pain, we began to praise and celebrate. I was still not sure what was happening, and I wondered whether the heat I had felt in my hands was just in my head, so I asked the woman what had just happened. She said she felt a lot of heat moving into her stomach from my hands. I barely had time to process these miraculous healings I just witnessed. We did take time to celebrate, giving all the glory to Jesus for what we had just witnessed. Later in the day, Darrin and I spoke with a woman who had come to the clinic because her upper back hurt her so much that she had difficulty sleeping. The woman had on a loose-fitting dress, and I could see a large bulge across her upper back. After she agreed to let me place both of my hands on her back, one in front of the other over the bulging area, I began to pray. Immediately, I felt the heat and then the waves move across her entire upper back. This time, the movement lasted longer than the previous two experiences. As Darrin continued to pray and I kept on thanking Jesus, I could sense the swelling in the woman's back shrinking.

As I prayed, it occurred to me that if the intensity of movement or waves I felt in my hands as I prayed was in any way related to the level of pain in the person I was praying over, it was clear that this woman was in a tremendous amount of pain. After the warmth and waves ended, the woman immediately began crying and began excitedly speaking to our interpreter. Darrin and I stood by helplessly as she continued to weep and speak to the interpreter. After a couple of minutes, I tried to interrupt her with an apology because I assumed the pain was still there. Tears started down my face as I told our interpreter that we could continue to pray for her. The interpreter paused his conversation with the woman and calmly held up a hand, indicating for me to hold on. After the woman stopped talking, the interpreter said that the woman had just told him that her pastor had prophesized that a woman with hot hands would heal her back the previous day in church. Her pain would be gone, and now it was. Hearing this, I was filled with so many emotions I needed to step away for a moment. I was so humbled and honored that Jesus would use Darrin's prayers and my hands to take away someone's pain. I had come on this trip to love little children, and today I was being used to heal. It was all too much for me to understand. For the remainder of the day, Darrin continued to lead in prayer, and I continued to lay my hands on the areas where people told me they felt pain. Not being the powerful prayer leader that Darrin was, I would simply whisper, "Thank you, Jesus" as I felt the heat and waves move through me and into the other person. The people we prayed over and laid hands on did not have access to medical care, so they could only let us know where the pain was, not what was causing it.

Darrin and I tried to pray over as many people in the clinic as time would allow, and even though we had missed a few, our tally sheet for the day was eighty-three. At the end of an exceptionally long and incredible day, I was told by one of the medics who had been here before that they expected to treat approximately one thousand citizens by the end of the mission.

One reason God was so faithful in healing his children of all ages was their tremendous faith and love for Christ. Following each healing, we raised our arms towards the sky and praised the Lord, giving Him the glory for what just happened. I made sure that, with every healing, our interpreter conveyed to the person I had prayed for that I knew that it was Jesus who performed the miraculous healing, I was simply His facilitator.

"Be still and know that I am God; I will be exalted among the nations, I will be exalted in the earth."
Psalm 46:10

4

Learning to Operate Under God's Power
His Will, Not Mine

I said goodbye to my mission partner and fantastic prayer warrior, Darrin, and began reflecting on all that I had experienced that day in the clinic. Thinking back through the first healing of the older woman with painful knees to each of the fantastic people I had the privilege of serving that day, I felt an incredible sense of joy sweep over me. If I could go back over that day and make one change, I would not. That day at the clinic, the incredible love I experienced reminded me of the love that I had heard people describe the feeling when they accepted Jesus into their hearts. In an instant, all my guilt, past hurts, failures, and feelings of being unworthy were swept away and replaced with an unfathomable love that was so true and pure that I knew it had to be Jesus. This incredible love I now know was my first love the Miracle Worker was working a miracle in my heart. I realized that, regardless how distant I'd felt from God, Jesus had never given up on me or left me. Jesus's love is unconditional, and although it may be difficult to fathom, He loved me more than anyone ever could, even my earthly parents. I walked away from the clinic a changed person. My heart had been healed. I now walked with a servant's heart that would continue to reveal God's love for His children. When I pray, saying "Thank you, Jesus" from my heart, it is enough, for He goes before me and knows all our needs. As I left the clinic, I asked the team if I could serve there again the next day. I had come to believe that being a part of the clinic team was what I was called to do. Serving in the clinic not only saved me, but also showed me the tremendous depth of trust, humility, and incredible faith and love for our Savior in those we prayed over. During my time spent with these amazing people who came to the clinic, I hugged each one. I could feel only genuine love and God's presence throughout the entire medical clinic!

That evening, my roommates and I were taking turns sharing our experiences of the day. I enjoyed listening to stories about all that occurred outside of the clinic at the other mission project sites with the beautiful people we were serving. When asked how my day went, I was excited to share the miraculous healings I had been honored to witness. I also shared my anticipation of being asked to serve in the clinic the next day. Before I drifted off to sleep that night, I wondered to myself why God would choose an ordinary woman like me to facilitate such remarkable healings. I began recalling stories I had heard through sermons of how Jesus often used ordinary people to do extraordinary things for His glory. The following morning, I was so excited as I prepared to spend another day in the medical clinic. At breakfast, I was approached by one of the mission leaders who told me that someone else in our group had requested to work in the clinic. The medical team had initially planned that they would each day have a different missionary from outside the medical team to serve with them, and then send someone from their medical team out in the field to serve. My heart sank I had truly believed I had been called to be a part of the clinic. But as disappointed as I was, I completely understood. My disappointment quickly turned to happiness as I realized that there would be people who needed prayers for healing in the neighborhoods and sports fields, as well as children to love.

The first person I met that day was a young girl who had been standing on the top bench of some bleachers between two other girls, all of whom appeared to be around the same age. As I walked across the soccer field, I waved at them, and they smiled and waved back. I felt led to make my way to them. Without an interpreter and with my limited Spanish, we laughed as I tried my best to communicate through words and made-up sign language. I understood that two of the girls were siblings ("mi hermana"), and the third girl was their cousin ("mi prima"). When I asked if any of them had pain ("¿Tienes dolor?"), the sweet girl in the middle replied "Si" and showed me she could only lift her left arm about halfway. I used gestures to ask if I could pray for her while I laid my hand on her arm, and she smiled and nodded yes. All four of us bowed our heads as I began thanking Jesus repeatedly, as I had done the day before.

Once again, I felt the heat and then those unusual waves moving in my hands. After the waves slowed then stopped, I removed my hands. The young girl slowly lifted her left arm over her head, then down, and then faster up and down again, like a bird flapping its wings. The young girls and I all celebrated, and I said "Gracias" as I pointed towards the sky. The young girls seem to understand and raised their arms to the sky in praise. As I sat with these precious girls, I did my best to convey how much Jesus loves them, by saying "Jesús te ama!" while pointing to the sky again, then tapping my heart and pointing to them. Smiling and nodding, the three little angels climbed down the bleachers and took off to run around the field, flapping their arms up and down and pretending to fly. Watching the girls run about and smile is a precious memory that will stay with me. After giving each of the girls a hug and saying goodbye, I started to head to a nearby neighborhood where some of the other missionaries were dancing to music with other children. On my way to join the other team members, I heard a child's laughter behind me. When I turned around, to my surprise, I saw the same little girl I had just laid hands on, still waving her arms up and down.

The little girl joined in the dancing with the other members of the missionary team and me. She was so happy to show me how she could move both her arms above her head as she danced about. Throughout the afternoon, I felt led by God to many other people, and he continued to use my gift of healing. I also joined my mission team group to entertain people with the dances and skits we had rehearsed in preparation for our trip. I enjoyed watching and occasionally participating with the kids playing sports in the fields, or just running around and loving them. I was so moved by their depth of faith and the amount of love they showed for our Heavenly Father and others. The people I met that day all seemed to have one thing in common: They had so few material possessions yet such incredible happiness. Each of them seemed so grateful for what little they had. As I thought about this, I was reminded of something my mother often said to my three sisters and me, "We may not have a lot of money or material possessions, but we are extremely rich because we have love, good health and especially each other."

"Lord my God, I called to you for help,
and you healed me."
Psalm 30:2

5

A Season of Favor to Know God Better

Operating Under God's Power

I had just finished laying my hands on a woman's lower back when one of the younger missionaries came running up to me. My first thought as he approached was that it was time to return to the hotel where we had been staying. We had made it a rule to always travel as a group for safety. Over the past few days, it was not uncommon for me to get so caught up talking with the people I was serving, that I would be the one of the last to catch up to the group. The team leaders and guides all knew my name by the end of the week because they were repeatedly checking to see if "Karen" was here before heading out. It was not my intention to make the group wait, but I just become so engrossed in serving that I would lose track of time until someone would come looking for me.

I could tell that this young man was not here to tell me it was time to go, because tears were running down his face. He had something more important to tell me. I figured out that he was saying something about a man who could not hear or talk. He and Rebecca, another missionary, on the team, had been praying for a deaf man for a while. I was being asked to join them. As I gathered up my things, the young man who was sent to find me kept repeating, "Cannot hear cannot talk, so please come now." Based on the urgency in his voice, I felt compelled to follow him without saying goodbye to my new friends immediately. The young man took my hand and started to lead me to one end of a sports field. I could see a group of people, and as I got closer, I saw Rebecca, the one who had prophesied to me about working in the medical clinic. She was praying over a man who I assumed was the man who could not hear or talk. Standing to the left of the man was a group of people who appeared to be his friends and family. When I reached the man who was deaf, the young man who had brought me there bent down and continued to pray passionately for the man. With his words "cannot talk, cannot hear" resonating through my head, I felt led to cup my hands over the man's ears and press my forehead to his.

I immediately felt heat in my hands as I began thanking Jesus. Within seconds of me starting to pray, I felt a hand on my back, then another. I began hearing a waterfall of prayer behind me as I continued thanking Jesus. I could hear more and more people praying behind me. I noticed that, as the prayers of others increased in numbers and volume, the heat and vibrations from my hands increased as well. The vibrations from my hands slowly intensified to the point that it took all my strength to continue to hold them over his ears. I sensed something huge was occurring.

When the vibration in my hands slowed to a stop, I put my hands down and stepped back while an interpreter asked the man if he could hear. He replied, "Ya." Some of those gathered around him, especially those who were standing to his side, started crying. The interpreter then asked him, "What is your name?" He said something that sounded like a name in Spanish. Speaking with his family, I was told that he had been born with his ear canals closed, and so he never heard and had never spoken until that moment. While everyone was celebrating, I realized that I would not have had the opportunity to be here for this miraculous healing had I served in the clinic that day. I then became aware of the significance of operating under God's power and will rather than my own.

During breakfast the following morning, as I walked by a table of mission team members, one of them looked at me and said, "Hey, you're that lady who laid hands on that man who was healed yesterday!" Turning towards him, I asked how he knew about it. He told me that he and some of the mission leaders had had some free time the previous day, so they drove around to see what the other missionaries were doing. He then picked up his phone and showed me photos that he had taken of me with my hands over the man's ears and a line of prayer warriors behind me.

"And my God will meet all of your needs according to His riches in glory in Christ Jesus."
Philippians 4:19

6

Our Amazing Interpreters
Breaking Barriers

The next few days of the mission trip were filled with becoming acquainted with more beautiful people living in the surrounding towns and villages. We were developing a routine of making sure our water bottles were filled and backpacks full of peanut butter sandwiches. Then, we would make pit stops between visiting neighborhoods and eat our peanut butter sandwiches. The fact that I could not share my peanut butter sandwiches made me feel sad knowing many of the family's were without food that day. During these lunch breaks, we would often do one of the skits we had rehearsed. The skits seemed to be moving even despite the language barrier, allowing our audience to receive the message of God's love and mercy. It seemed that there were no barriers when it came to expressing and sharing love. It was evident that God's presence was everywhere.

God continued to lead me to people in need of healing and was faithful to take their pain away, and He always sent me an interpreter just when I needed one. With the help of an interpreter, we were able to share prayers and testimonies easily. The interpreters I had the privilege to work with were such a big part of what we were doing. For example, Sarabelle and Francisco, a brother-and-sister team, also became my brother and sister in Christ, like the rest of the fantastic interpreters we worked with. I keep in touch with most of them to this day. Another sweet interpreter named Dania shared that she suffered from chronic headaches caused by a head injury she had sustained as a child. One day when Dania and I were together, she said she had a terrible headache. I decided to take a moment and simply lay my hands on her head. I could immediately feel the heat building in my hands and what felt like circular motions coming from my hands. After a few minutes, she said the pain was gone. Dania was very young, and I felt a tremendous sense of compassion for her. I often sat with her on the bus as we traveled from village to village.

During our time on the bus, I learned that she and her mother made bracelets that they sold to pay their rent. Knowing Dania's story and seeing how beautiful the bracelets were, I had to purchase several as souvenirs. One day, before we exited the bus, I kissed Dania's forehead, and she glanced up at me and smiled, then asked me why I had done that. I told her she reminded me of a daughter.

Dania shared with me that it is the highest form of adoration in the Dominican Republic when an adult kisses a child on the forehead. I had indeed come to adore Dania, and since then, I have made it a point to kiss my grandbabies on the forehead every chance I get, and I have shared with them what Dania told me such a kiss symbolizes. One of my precious grandbabies is also prone to randomly getting debilitating chronic headaches. Seeing what God had done for Dania, I decided to lay my hands one of my grandchildren. Within minutes of laying my hands on them, my hands became warm, and I began to feel that same circular motion. Thanking Jesus as my grandchild felt the pain leaving their body, my grandchild rose within minutes, exhibiting the typical unbridled energy of child. From that day on whenever I say, "Do

not forget to thank Jesus," a child's voice always replies,
"I already did, Nani!".

"Now all glory to God, who is able, through his mighty
power at work within us, to accomplish infinitely more
than we might ask or think"
Ephesians 3:20 (NLT)

7

Radiant Reyna
"Bless You!"

Our week in the Dominican Republic seemed to go by too quickly, and as Friday approached, our final mission project was to distribute five hundred pairs of shoes that our church had donated. This event took place on a fenced field with benches lined up on one side of the fencing. As I was waiting on one of the benches, I recognized one of our medics, Andy, coming slowly towards me with a woman who was walking slightly bent over. When they reached where I was sitting, Andy asked if I could pray with him for the woman. Andy had been volunteering in the medical clinic during the week. As a veterinary technician, he had a tremendous amount of medical knowledge. Andy introduced the woman as Reyna Marte; she lived outside of Puerto Plata. Reyna had approached Andy with a letter from her doctor stating which vertebrae in her lower back were injured from a car accident, and she was hoping to find some relief. As I sat with Reyna, I could see that her inner beauty matched her outer beauty.

Not fully understanding human anatomy, I asked Andy and her for guidance on where to place my hands for her to receive healing. Andy and I began to pray over her, thanking Jesus. Almost immediately, I felt heat waves moving from my hands into Reyna's back. As the movement seemed to cease, I slid my hand up to the middle of Reyna's back, where it met Andy's hand, and once again, I felt the heat and movement in my hands. When the waves stopped, Andy and I removed our hands. Reyna immediately stood up perfectly straight and began repeating, "No pain!" Watching her jump up and down and she stretched her hands towards the heavens gave me such joy.

Andy and I celebrated with her. I was amazed at God's divine appointment of bringing together Andy and Reyna and then placing us all in the same place for another miracle to occur. Andy, Reyna, and I continued to talk for a while until it was time for us to set up the shoe distribution. After sorting through the shoes and organizing them by size, we all spread out, each with our bowl of water and towels to wash the feet of so many precious children before fitting them with brand new shoes. As I washed each child's feet, I was reminded of a story in the Bible, in the thirteenth chapter of John, where Jesus humbled Himself by washing the disciples' feet. In the early Christian church, washing others' feet was a sign of humility and selfless love, and I felt honored to be doing it for these children. After putting the shoes on the children's feet, they danced around the sports field as if they were wearing golden slippers.

Now, whenever I see a child wearing a pair of shoes, I visualize those children in the Dominican Republic with their beautiful, proud faces. For some of those children, these were the only shoes they would own. As the day ended and we were packing up the few shoes left, I heard a voice on the other side of the field shouting, "Bless you!" "Bless you!" in my direction. When I looked up, I saw the head of a young boy popping up and down. He was jumping up, trying to see over the fence that surrounded the field. When he saw me looking at him, he held up one of the pair of shoes we had just passed out.

I was confused, thinking maybe he needed a different size, but after showing me the shoes, he started pointing towards the ground. It was then that I noticed two heads were popping up and down. He pointed to the second boy and then to the shoes. It became clear that he was there to help his friend, who must have missed getting a pair of shoes. The young boy indicated that his friend needed the same size as his. I searched through a nearby duffel bag of shoes until I found the correct size, and when I did, I tossed them over the fence with all my might to be sure to get them to the boys. As they caught the shoes, an expression of gratitude and excitement filled their faces, followed by one more "Bless you!" Seeing how the boys watched over each other was another reminder of how deeply the people here cared for each other.

"Lord my God, I called to you for help,
and you healed me"
Psalm 30:2

8

The Celebration
A Nation's Transformation

The closing celebration of our week was hosted at a local stadium, which slowly became filled with mission team members from around the world. Just seconds before our team walked onto the field, Andy turned to me and pointed up to where Reyna was standing up in the bleachers, waving her arms in the air. As we waved back, she moved her hands up and down her sides, mouthing the words "No pain, no pain!" As we all worshiped to praise music during the celebration, I occasionally glanced up at Reyna and saw her praising and dancing to the music, radiant in her red dress. The celebration of 1Nation1Day, the mission trip's name, took place in twenty different venues in twenty different states across the Dominican Republic. Thousands of

Dominicans and missionaries joined together as witnesses of this amazing transformation in stadiums and on television across the country. As I looked around at everyone celebrating, my heart was overflowing with joy and love. I knew at this moment that falling back in love with Jesus was the best decision I had ever made. The most surprising miracle was not in what happens to others but in what happens to me.

As I reflect on my first international mission trip, I become overwhelmed with the power of the Holy Spirit in the lives of those who believe in Him. The people we served had so little in terms of material goods, but they possessed tremendous faith and love for Jesus and others. This experience was life-changing for me: I was finally reunited with Jesus Christ, who thankfully never gave up on me, even though it took fifty-four years for me to find my way back to Him. As I left the Dominican Republic, my heart was consumed with love for Him, and I desired to know Him on a more intimate level. I felt so humbly blessed to be used as a vessel for physical healings of such devoted followers of Jesus. And I realized that His divine appointments were as much a miracle as the healings themselves.

As a result of that unforgettable week, I came to know more deeply that God is so good and faithful, and He does what He says He will do. When I accepted Jesus as my Savior, I was anointed by the Holy Spirit with His holy fire. Regardless of how good or knowledgeable you are, you must receive Christ as your personal savior to receive His gift of living eternally with Him. His unconditional love for me is now what determines the lifestyle I strive to live.

"Let each of you look out not only for your interests, but also for the interests of others."
Philippians 2:4 (NKJV)

9

Finding a Home Church
for Healings
Love Fellowship Worship Center

When I returned home from the Dominican Republic and settled back into life in New York, I felt called to find a church where healings were a part of the worship service. I was curious to see if Jesus had used me for healings in the Dominican Republic only because those, I laid hands on did not have access to medical care, or if he would continue to use me for healings regardless of where I was.

One day, I was talking with a coworker that everyone calls "Brother Bob." Brother Bob's love for Jesus was so strong and clear, and he freely shared his faith and the gospel through prison ministry and his gospel blues band,

Light Blue. Brother Bob and his fellow musicians would minister through music in various venues. Bob also played on the worship team at a church called Love Fellowship Worship Center (LFWC). As I shared some of the miracles, I had witnessed on my mission trip, his eyes grew wide, and he shared that he had been praying for the gift of healing. I mentioned that I was searching for a church that was open to healings, and he invited me to visit his home church, which not only facilitated healings, but even had a prayer room that is often used for healings. I was particularly intrigued by LFWC because I wanted to learn more about the gift of healing within the church, and I did not recall witnessing healings in the previous churches I had attended.

I felt immediately welcomed during my first visit to LFWC. True to its name, everyone at LFWC was genuinely loving as I made my way into the sanctuary. I found a spot in the second row of seats near where Brother Bob was waiting to begin leading worship. Shortly after the service began, I noticed a man walk by and sit in the row of seats in front of me. Once worship started, that man, and Pastor Cooper, stood up. As he preached, he walked back and forth, remaining at eye level with the congregation. His message was that a pastor is no better than his flock, so he should stand among them, not above them. His wife, Terri, who read a scripture at the beginning of the service, had seated herself alongside us in the second row of pews. Humility is a quality that is important to me, so seeing the way Pastor Cooper and his wife acted made me feel I had found the church in which God wanted me to worship and serve.

At the end of the service, Pastor Cooper asked us to take hold of the persons' hands to our left and right so that we could pray for each other. I reached across the aisle and took hold of the woman's hand on my right, and then reached forward to take hold of the hand of a man sitting in front of me. The moment I grabbed his hand, I started to feel a sense of heat, then movement, similar to what I had experienced in the Dominican Republic. I wondered if that was a sign that I would be facilitating healings in this church.

As everyone was making their way downstairs for fellowship after the service, I held back and waited for a few minutes. After the congregation left the sanctuary, Pastor Cooper walked up to welcome me and introduced himself. I explained to him who had invited me to church and why. As we continued to talk, I sensed that Pastor James not only understood but expected the gift of healing. I then mentioned that I had felt the same heat and wave-like sensation when I held the man's hand in front of me as I had felt during healings on my mission trip. Pastor Cooper asked me to come with him for a moment and grabbed my hand. While leading me quickly downstairs, he grabbed a baby carrier from a mother who was also heading downstairs, carried it down for her, then carefully set it down and continued leading me down a hall. Pastor Cooper led me right up to the man who had been sitting in front of me earlier. Catching my breath, I looked the man directly in the eyes and asked the same question I had asked countless times through interpreters in the Dominican Republic, "Do you have pain?" Geno, the man who Pastor Cooper had led me to, said "Yes!" and shared with me that his knees were bad, which was why he had to sit during the entire service. Geno continued to tell me about the nerve damage in his hand, showing me how he could not make a fist. I asked Geno if he would give me permission to lay hands on him and pray for him. As soon as I placed my hands over his

51

knees, the heat began to build and flow. While I was thanking Jesus for the healing that would occur in his name, Brother Bob laid his hand on my shoulder, and others also joined us in the room. Soon, Geno soon began alternating between standing and sitting. The pain was gone from his knees. I then held his hands in mine and felt the heat and wave-like sensation while thanking Jesus for the healing that was to occur. This time when the heat and waves stopped, Geno started to open and close his hand and wiggle his fingers. He remarked that, although he could not believe how much more flexible his hand was, I still felt that something was undone. I felt led to slide my right hand over the left side of his lower back, and the prayer warriors around us continued praying and praising. I felt heat under my hands start up again. Geno had not mentioned pain in his back, but somehow, I knew I was not done. Geno also didn't elaborate on what was causing his back pain, but he seemed to be feeling better after we finished praying for him. Later, as I met and spoke with others in the church fellowship room, I started to feel that this could, indeed, be my new place of worship and a place for me to see miracles.

"But because of His great love for us, God, who is rich in mercy, made us alive with Christ even when we were dead in transgressions t is by grace you have been saved."
Ephesian 4:4-5

10

His Amazing Ways
A Supernatural Revelation

Geno, who was a good friend of Brother Bob, told me before I left after that first visit that, when he had first seen me walk into church and did not recognize me, he decided to sit in front of me so that he could greet me after the service. Another great divine appointment. I had no initial inclination that God had placed Geno and me in each other's lives, but as time passed, God used us to do amazing things together, and soon I was calling Geno a brother in Christ.

Soon after my visit to LFWC, I received a call from Brother Bob that Geno was in the hospital. Geno had gone to the hospital because he thought he had a heart attack. It turned out to be bronchitis. On Tuesday, Geno called to tell me not only about his condition, but that he had something incredible to share with me: His doctor had asked him, "What have been doing? Your kidneys now look perfectly healthy!" Even though his kidneys had been in rough shape before I had prayed for his healing, they had not hurt, so Geno had not thought to mention them when I asked if he was in pain anywhere else. God knew where he needed healing, and the Holy Spirit guided my hands and voice to heal all of Geno that day. Geno was convinced that God had healed his kidneys. As I thought about this revelation, I realized that I had only asked if he had pain. In the Dominican Republic, since most people lacked proper medical diagnoses, they only knew something was wrong if they felt pain. I have now learned to ask more in-depth questions regarding people's need for healing. And I have learned to trust when I feel called to lay my hands someplace other than where someone has indicated.

Today, I am an active member of LFWC and facilitate physical healings when called to. Love Fellowship Worship Center is a very fitting name for this church: Everyone there is so welcoming and loving towards each other, and they raise the roof as they worship. During sermons, I hang on to every word the pastor says, and at times I feel as though he is speaking directly into my life. In this church, some fantastic prayer warriors have become sisters in Christ. They and the rest of the parishioners are always more than willing to pray over anyone in need.

One day, I was invited to spend the day with the prayer warriors' team. The plan was to go around the city and pray over people in need of healing. I was excited to come alongside these selfless ladies and be a member of the body of Christ acting in the community. We started by meeting at one of the team members' homes, where we prayed for healing and peace before going into the community. I loved how the prayer warriors prayed with every fiber of their being. One of people we visited that day was a woman who suffered terrible hip pain. When we entered her home, we were met by a family member, Sabrina, who apologetically told us that she was suffering from a migraine and would not be participating in praying over her mother-in-law. Sabrina's mother-in-law was sitting in a chair, and she explained that she had a lot of pain in her hips. I knelt and slid my hands between her hips and the inside of the chair. As I began to thank Jesus for this healing, I could feel a lot of heat and motion moving through my hands. As I kept thanking Jesus and the prayer warriors joined me in prayer, after a couple of minutes, I felt a hand on my shoulder. When the heat and motion stopped in my hands, I turned around and saw that the hands belonged to Sabrina, who said with excitement, "My migraine is gone!" The Holy Spirit had not only healed her mother-in-law's hips, but also taken away Sabrina's migraine.

"For prophecy never had its origin in the will of man, but men spoke from God as they were carried along by the Holy Spirit."
2 Peter 1:21

11

¡Yo Soy Mas!
I Am More!

Worshipping with my new sisters and brothers in Christ at LFWC, I began preparing for my second mission trip with 1Nation1Day. This trip would take me to Honduras for a week during the summer of 2016. As I prepared for the trip, I worked full-time as a teacher and part-time as a youth and family advocate. Both jobs were equally rewarding and afforded me the opportunity to self-fund my upcoming trip.

On this trip, I would be joining a group of people from all over the United States. Our group would be going to Honduras to follow up a previous mission group, which had focused on violence against women. As a result of that group's impact, the government of Honduras had asked 1Nation1Day to come back. Our group would be visiting sixteen schools during the week, where we would be working with teachers and students, and praying with them to have a relationship with Jesus and help end violence against women.

The goal of the first 1Nation1Day mission trip to Honduras was simply to bring hope and change by coming alongside and ministering to the people of Honduras. The goal of this second 1Nation1Day mission trip was inspired by the prophet Isaiah's words, "Can a country be born in a day or a nation be brought forth in a moment?" (Isaiah 66:8). The answer is "Yes." I know this to be true because the 1Nation1Day first mission team had been the largest-ever sent to Honduras, consisting of approximately two thousand missionaries. That group influenced over 250,000 students, through prayer, skits and dramas, to pursue their dreams and follow Jesus. On this second trip, 1Nation1Day would include medical personnel, and we would distribute two million meals and one hundred thousand shoes, with a focus on providing physical and spiritual healing. During the first trip, almost five hundred thousand people in eighteen stadiums across Honduras had come together to celebrate the new

Honduras. If the first 1Nation1Day could have that kind of impact, I knew I was in for something amazing.

"'But I will restore you to health and heal your wounds,' declares the LORD."
Jeremiah 30:17

12

Brother Bob's Unexpected Miracles
God's Power is Limitless

While I was preparing to travel to Honduras, I felt led to pray for Brother Bob after the church service one Sunday. I believed that God had decided it was Bob's time for a miracle. As Bob was packing up his guitar, I asked him if he could meet with me and some prayer warriors in the prayer room to pray over someone. Bob readily agreed and even invited Vu and Mercy, who he knew had a powerful gift of prayer, to join us. Although I did not know precisely what type of healing Bob needed, I knew the Holy Spirit would guide my hands, as well as our prayers. When we were all gathered in the prayer room, Brother Bob asked who we were praying for, and we told him, "You." I asked Brother Bob what he felt we were called together to pray over, Bob asked if we could pray over his bipolar disorder. As the prayer warriors began to pray, Bob sat in a chair, and I stood behind him and placed my hands on his head. I immediately felt heat and a sense of movement in my hands. As we were praying, Bob shared that he had been struggling with bipolar disorder for over twenty years. I continued to thank Jesus, as the women prayed with every fiber of their being. After the movement and heat ceased in my hands, I lifted them and could see my faint pink handprints on the top of his bald head. I had never before facilitated the brain's healing, so at the time I was not sure what was happening or what to expect. Brother Bob was grateful for the prayers and thanked us, and shared that he had felt the heat from my hands.

A few weeks later, I received a call from Bob, he told me that he had lost his insurance coverage for his bipolar medication and could not afford the $900-a-month prescription. But then he shared that he had been off his medication for approximately three weeks and had been feeling even better than when he had been taking the medication! Not only had the medication made it difficult to concentrate, but now he could drink coffee again. He also said that, when Vu, Mercy, and I prayed over him, the heat and waves of movements he had felt all over the top of his head had actually stayed with him for a brief time. I was beyond amazed and so happy for Bob's healing. Bob is so humble and a selfless servant to everyone he meets. His healing helped confirm to me that nothing is too big for God, the greatest physician of all. Even Bob's excitement about being able to enjoy coffee again was a reminder that God delights when we appreciate even the little things. Bob sees his coffee as one the best gift of his healing!

A few years later, he asked if I would pray and lay hands on his daughter Kim and granddaughter Kiya. Both were believers and had faith that Jesus could perform miracles. Kiya had been having pain in her right knee, and her mother, Kim, had pain in her hip and lower back. After setting a day and time to meet, I arrived at their home and was greeted by Bob and two of the sweetest girls I have had the pleasure of meeting. After we all spent some time getting acquainted, Bob and I started praying over Kiya and then Kim. I placed my hand over Kiya's knee, and immediately I felt heat then movement flowing through my hand. When the movement ceased, I lifted my hand, and Kiya stood up and said the pain was gone. Next, I asked Kim to tell me when I had my hand over where the pain was on her right hip and lower back. When Kim told me I had located the spot, Bob began to pray as I began thanking Jesus. After what seemed like minutes, I could feel something shift under my hand over her hip. It felt like cartilage or bone moving. I asked Kim if she also felt a bone moving, and she said "Yes" and that the pain was gone. This shifting-of-bone sensation was new to me. I recently talked with Bob, and he said the girls are still pain-free and exercising regularly. Just as their earthly father, Bob, was happy for his children to be healed, I believe our father in heaven rejoices when any of his children receive a miracle.

"The Spirit himself bears witness with our spirit that we are children of God"
Romans 8:16

13

US Returns to Honduras
A Very Important Mission

When it was finally time to go on my second mission trip, I was excited to be among the beautiful people of Honduras who would soon become brothers and sisters in Christ. I could not wait to love them, give them a message of hope, and share with them about how they could have a personal relationship with Jesus. This time, as I waited with my mission team in the Miami airport to board our flight to Honduras, I gripped my passport tightly in my hand.

Honduran President Juan Orlando Hernández and First Lady Ana García de Hernández had invited 1Nation1Day back to help the people of Honduras combat violence against women through education and salvation, and by instilling in women, girls, men and boys that women have value. At the time of our arrival, more than 26 percent of Honduran women and girls had reported abuse by men at some point of their lives. This trip was called "Yo Soy Mas" (I am more), affirming that each woman has infinite worth and value. Prior to coming together in Miami right before our trip, each member of the team had rehearsed through virtual training a number of skits and dances we would be performing. On this trip, our team leaders were Rachael and Jessica, who were spiritually invested in this mission trip and in each of us. I breathed a sigh of relief as the plane took off, and I could hardly contain my excitement regarding what the week would hold for us. After we settled into where we would be staying in Honduras, we were introduced to a group of incredible interpreters, and then had the opportunity to get to know our fellow missionaries better. My assignment on this trip was to visit schools and witness to students and staff.

I would team up with different interpreters each day. One of my interpreters, Mario, was a faithful servant of God and had a gift for relating with youth. I also teamed up with two other interpreters, both named Alejandro. Often when we entered a school, we would feel led by

God to a particular individual or group of students in need of prayer. I was touched by how often the children would ask for prayer for someone other than themselves, such as a brother, sister, or parent. I recall one young boy who, with tears flowing down his cheeks, asked us to pray for his grandmother, who was very sick. I prayed with him and later was told by a teacher that he had lost his parents, so his grandmother was all the family he had. I talked to the students about Jesus, telling them how much he loved each of them and that he had paid for their salvation. On one occasion, Mario and I felt led to approach a group of students sitting with their heads bowed. We were not sure if they were trying to avoid us, but when we asked them if we could pray for them, they lifted up their heads, and many of them had tears in their eyes. We began praying as they bowed their heads again. I was excited to see that many of them had Bibles in their book bags as part of their curriculum. I also was happy to see how quickly the students bonded to Mario, and his love for them was evident as well. It was clear during this visit that God uses us for spiritual healings as well as physical. Some of the conversations we had and healings we witnessed were in the schools, while a few were with people waiting in line outside the medical clinic.

I recall one mother holding a baby and holding the hand of her young daughter. Through one of the interpreters, this mother told me that her baby had something protruding out of her chest, and her other daughter had frequent headaches. The mother allowed me to cradle her precious baby, and as I laid my hand over her chest, I felt a bump that felt like a hernia. As I began to pray for the child, I felt the heat start to move through my hands. As I prayed and watched, I could see the swelling slowly going down. Before the healing heat stopped moving through my hands, I placed the mother's hand under my own, so she could feel the miracle occurring. When we finished praying, and the mother and I removed our hands, the baby seemed at such peace. I could only give God all the glory. I then placed my hand gently on her daughter's head and started thanking Jesus immediately. I felt the heat begin to move through my hands and into the little girl. As this was occurring, the little girl stood very still with her eyes closed. After the heat and movement stopped in my hand, the interpreter asked if the little girl's headache was gone. She replied with a smile and nodded her head yes. We explained to her that the heat she had felt was from the Holy Spirit sent by God.

"Jesus looked at them and said, 'With man this is impossible, but with God all things are possible.'"
Matthew 19:26

14

Curing the Incurable
My Sister Bri and Kate

No matter the mission trip, lunch always seemed to be the same: peanut butter and jelly sandwiches. With each peanut butter sandwich, I quickly realized how fortunate I was to have the guarantee of never going hungry or thirsty. Food and clean water were things that many of those we served prayed for. Breakfast was different. Each morning we would start with a fantastic breakfast and end our day with a delicious dinner. However, after each of these big meals it upset me to watch people toss leftovers in the trash after we had spent time among those who had so little.

One missionary team member with us on the trip, Kate, had celiac disease, which is incurable and requires a strict gluten-free diet. Celiac inhibits the small intestine's ability to process gluten properly, making eating food that contains gluten difficult and painful. One evening during dinner, we were served a spicy meal. Kate was served an alternative meal to avoid triggering her celiac, and it was unappetizingly bland. I was seated at a table at the opposite end of the dining room and heard Kate call out to me, "Hey Karen! That looks good, and I want some, so could you come and lay your hand on my stomach?" At that moment, I believe it was her faith that spurred me on to immediately leave my chair, walk to where she was sitting and lay my hand on her stomach while thanking Jesus. Almost immediately, we both felt heat and waves of movement. After the heat faded and the waves ended, Kate ate the regular, spicy meal and did not become ill. I recently had a conversation with her about this miracle, and she told me she still is cured of celiac disease.

I believe anything can be fixed when you trust Jesus, who is the greatest physician. God has placed so many beautiful people in my life, as far back as I can remember. Therefore, it did not surprise me that although most of the missionaries in our group did not know each other before joining the mission, by the end of the week, we had all become brothers and sisters in Christ. Bri and I had developed a remarkably close relationship by the end of our mission trip. Bri was diagnosed with cerebral palsy at seven months and depended on a walker to walk. I was amazed by the love and compassion Bri had for others, and especially impressed with her enduring relationship with Jesus. Many of us prayed over Bri that week for healing. We did see some improvement in her health as she began to walk independently of the walker for a short distance. As much as I wanted Bri to be wholly healed, I realized that healings are not always instant. Some healings are works in progress, while others will have to wait for heaven. I also was asked to pray over and lay hands on two beautiful and devoted daughters of God suffering from advanced cancer. Although they were not fully healed, they all shared with me that they were filled with a peace that may have been used to prepare them for their journey to heaven, where they know that God will bring them home to be healed. Although my heart was broken for these ladies' loved ones, I was so happy for these precious women of God. I genuinely believe they are now forever at peace, surrounded by eternal, unconditional love and joy.

"So do not fear, for I am with you; be not dismayed, for I am your God. I will strengthen you and help you; I will uphold you with my righteous right hand."
Isaiah 41:10

15

With Miracles, Everything is Possible! Open Door Mission

After returning from another fantastic mission trip and being a part of an even larger family in Christ, I decided to make LFWC my official home church. I had fallen in love with LFWC's parishioners and the services. On more than one Sunday, Pastor James spoke so specifically into my life that I knew God was speaking through him. Each Sunday, I could be found sitting in the front next to Geno and his brother, Kelly.

Geno and I had become close friends, so I was not surprised when he called me one day. What did surprise me was when Geno asked me if I could pray for his daughter, Courtney, who had lost her eyesight from glaucoma. I gladly agreed to pray for her. I asked Geno whether he would bring his daughter to church, or if wanted me to go to her. Geno replied that Courtney could not come to church because she lived in Florida. Geno then said, "I thought that after church this week, you, Brother Bob, and I could go somewhere and pray over her picture." I agreed, even though this would be a first for me. Geno was so confident and had such incredible faith that I thought *Why not?* The following Sunday, after the service, Geno and Bob and I went to a nearby restaurant. The restaurant was quite busy, and Geno chose a table in the middle of the other tables. Being in such an environment during a discussion of healing was out of my comfort zone. Fortunately, when I pray for healing, my focus is only on what I am sensing and thanking Jesus to facilitate healing. After we all settled in, we decided to pray over Courtney's picture first, and then eat. Geno pulled up a picture of Courtney on his phone, and I placed my right hand over Courtney's photo.

Geno and Bob took turns praying as I continually thanked Jesus. I was surprised when I felt heat coming from my hand and small waves as I held my hand over the phone. Somehow, I expected things to be different because I had placed my hand on a phone, not a person. When I felt what seemed like the end of the heat waves, we sat down, thanking Jesus, and settled into a nice lunch. I received a call from Geno, who said, "Guess what! I called my daughter this morning and told her that a faith healer, Bob, and I had prayed over her picture after church for healing." Geno's daughter replied that she could see clearly when she had opened her eyes that morning! It was so great to be able to celebrate this miracle with Geno. I was beyond happy for Courtney, and I felt that Jesus had given not only her sight but her life back. Courtney's healing reminded me that the Holy Spirit is everywhere, and he can answer the prayers of one person for another even when we are in different states. The Holy Spirit was with us and with Courtney while we prayed for her healing. From that point on, whenever I am asked to pray for someone and cannot be with them, I try to get a photo of them on my phone to pray over.

Once a month, Brother Bob's Christian blues band, Light Blue, would lead a praise and worship service at a Christian homeless shelter called Open Door Mission. During these services, I would join Geno and others to pray for anyone who wanted to receive salvation and healing. Many times during these visits, we witnessed instant healing from pain. Many of the homeless men also would ask for prayers for their family members. Even when I had no family member's photograph to lay my hands on, I felt led to lay my hand on the area where the man said his loved one needed healing. Many of these individuals would later share with me that their loved ones were healed. More and more, through those miraculous healings I saw how Jesus has a compassionate heart for the poor and oppressed. In John 16:17, Jesus promised his twelve apostles that if he went away, he would send the Advocate, the Holy Spirit, but if He stayed, the Holy Spirit could not come. The Holy Spirit is everywhere at all times. There are many gifts from the Holy Spirit, one of which is the gift of healing. The purpose of these gifts is to lead non-believers to Christ as He reveals Himself through those gifts.

"In their hearts humans plan their course, but the Lord establishes their steps."
Proverbs 16:9

16

Nicaragua with Bri
Ministering with Matheuw

Bri and I kept in touch after we arrived back home from our Honduras mission trip. In the fall of 2016, she asked me if I wanted to be her mission partner with her South Eastern University (SEU) 1Nation1Day mission trip to Nicaragua. I accepted the invitation. Bri and I agreed to spend time together with my Florida family for a few days before leaving for Nicaragua. We had a wonderful time in Florida and grew even closer. My loving, generous family embraced Bri, quickly welcoming her as part of the family. I was grateful to have this time to get to know Bri on a more personal level. She continued to amaze me with the depth of her faith and her tremendous love for others and Jesus. I was so grateful for my family and their wonderful hospitality, as well as for the opportunity to rest up for another exciting mission trip.

After hearing about the significant changes that had taken place in Honduras with 1National1Day, Nicaragua had contacted Missions.Me, the organization that coordinates 1Nation1Day mission trips. As a result, Missions.Me planned several seven-day mission trips across seventeen states in seventeen stadiums and fields across Nicaragua. On this Missions.Me trip, local business leaders and politicians gathered in different venues to prepare for three thousand missionaries to come together from five continents to help their nation implement changes that would impact many generations. The trip's primary mission was to combat poverty, as Nicaragua is the second poorest country in the Western Hemisphere.

On our first mission day, Bri and I were paired up with a young interpreter named Matheuw, a Nicaragua citizen. As a team, we were granted permission to go through the neighborhoods seeking people in need of healing. Matheuw appeared very compassionate and had a heart for others. The first person to be healed was a woman who, like many we would encounter, had had pain in her stomach for a long time. This woman showed me where to place my hand and, to my surprise, when I asked Matheuw to pray, he broke out in a beautiful song. I immediately felt the heat and movement between my hand and her stomach begin. When the sensation between us quieted, the lady raised her hands to the sky, giving glory to Jesus. Bri, Matheuw, and I visited many neighborhoods and were always welcomed with a warm embrace. All the people we prayed over or laid hands on were so gracious and welcomed us into their homes. Many homes were small structures with dirt floors and often housed more than one family. As we visited with each family, I was intrigued by how happy they appeared and how they treated us like their own.

Matheuw was the first person I had ever encountered who prayed by singing. I found it to be so calming and beautiful. I was curious what the lyrics were. Matheuw told me the songs he sang were about healing. The song he said he sang the most is called "Yo Se Que Estas Aqui." The English translation is "I know you are here [God]." As soon as he began singing, he said he could feel the presence of God move among us. All of Matheuw's songs were about faith that God could heal, restore, strengthen and give a new opportunity to people, and that if the people had faith in God, He could grant them miracles.

"Now to each one the manifestation of the Spirit is given for the common good."
1 Corinthians 12:7

17

Return to Honduras
Families That Pray Together

Serving on these life-changing mission trips had been such a blessing that I had a desire to travel to Honduras as often as I could. Since Mario and I had established such a wonderful friendship, I asked him if he would have time to minister with me if I could arrange travel to Honduras again. Mario agreed, as long we could work around his school schedule. We decided to plan our trip for July, when I would fly into his hometown of San Pedro Sula and stay for a week.

I was excited to serve again in Honduras with Mario. Although I loved being a part of the larger mission trips in which different countries came together to help their host country, this time I looked forward to discovering what God had planned for our little mission trip of two.

Mario met me at the airport, and then took me to my hotel so I could get settled. After catching up with Mario, I was excited to discover that he had ministered in many places that we would be visiting over the next few days. Mario's knowledge of the area afforded us access to the public hospital and the orphanages. Mario suggested that we visit the public hospital on the first day.

The following morning, Mario picked me up at the hotel, and we headed to the public hospital. After parking, we walked towards a large public building that had people of all ages sitting and standing all around it. Mario explained that many of the people outside the building were family members of those in the hospital or those hoping to get a bed in the hospital. There were also many people sitting and sleeping on cots in the open courtyard. These people were too poor to travel back and forth each day to visit hospitalized family members, so instead, they simply camped out in the courtyard. Mario and I had agreed earlier in the day to allow God to lead us to whomever we should serve. Mario turned to me and said, "I feel we should go to her," while gesturing toward an elderly woman who was sitting on a wall facing the hospital. As we approached the elderly woman, Mario began to speak with her in Spanish. Mario told me that her husband, Gregordio, had been run over by a taxi driver, and his leg had been broken in two places. He needed an operation so that he could walk again. The elderly lady told Mario that the taxi driver said he would be back with money to cover her husband's surgery. Like so many others, she could not afford to travel between her home and the hospital, so she had been sleeping on a cot outside in the courtyard, where she could see the window of her husband's hospital room. Mario explained that taxi drivers do not have to carry insurance, and this driver would likely not come through with the money for surgery. Mario knew some of the medics, so we were allowed to visit Gregordio's room along with his wife.

The inside of the hospital was very different from what I am used to in the US. As we made our way up to Gregordio's room, I noticed that most rooms had four beds, and the hospital appeared to be fully occupied. Once we entered Gregordio's room, we introduced ourselves and asked if we could pray for him. He agreed, but told us that he was deaf in one ear and asked us to stand on his good ear's side. Instead, I placed my hand over his deaf ear and began to thank Jesus repeatedly. In my hands I felt heat and a slight vibration. When I stopped praying, Gregordio looked over at me and said that he could hear again. He then showed us an x-ray of his leg, which clearly showed where the breaks were. I carefully placed a hand over each area where the break appeared to be while Mario prayed over him. I could feel the sensations of movement and heat building in my hands, and when it all stopped, Gregordio said the pain in his leg had subsided. He then shared that he knew someone was coming to heal him because, the day before, a pastor had told him that two people would be coming to help him heal. When it was time to go, Mario and I assured Gregordio and his wife that we would be back. Mario and I walked with his wife and Gregordio's his son, Martin, back to where they were staying in the hospital courtyard. Before leaving for the day, we made sure their family had something to drink and eat.

The rest of the day, Mario drove me around to show me some of the sights before heading back to the hotel. The next day, Mario and I went back to the hospital as promised. Gregordio's wife and Martin were waiting in the same spot in the courtyard, and we all went to Gregordio's room to check on him. Gregordio was very happy to see us, and excited to share with us that he had been able to stand for a short time after we'd left the previous day. He also said that he saw an angel flying above our heads as he had watched us leave. I have always been fascinated with angels and love to hear stories of angel encounters. I was taught that humans do not become angels, but angels can take on human form to serve as God's messengers. The Bible also talks a lot about guardian angels. As a young girl, I was taught that each of us is assigned a guardian angel at birth to help guide and protect us throughout our life. Knowing I will always have a guardian angel brings me such peace and confidence.

"Every good gift and perfect gift is from above, coming down from the Father of the heavenly lights, who does not change with shifting shadows."
James 1:17

18

Gratitude Abounds
Heartbreaking Sacrifices

Before leaving the hotel area for the day one morning, I stopped by a small boutique with beautiful clothing. I bought a few items that I thought Gregordio wife would appreciate. During my last hospital visit with Gregordio, I had an opportunity to be alone with him and felt compelled to lay hands on him one more time. While I laid my hands over where the breaks in his legs were, I felt a shift, as if his bones were coming together. Confused about what had just happened, I decided to pay for an x-ray of his legs. Looking at the x-ray, I could see that there were no longer any discernable breaks in his leg. Gregordio told me he had felt the shift as well. During our visit, the doctors who had scheduled his leg surgery came in to do a preop exam, and asked me to please step out of the room. I left the room, but stood just outside his doorway, where I could see them. While the doctors were moving and bending Gregordio's leg, I watched his face for any indication of pain. After the doctors left, I returned to the room and asked Gregordio if he had felt any pain when the doctors were moving his leg. Gregordio said no. At the end of the week, as I said my final goodbye to Gregordio and his beautiful family, I was thrilled to receive a photo of his family from Mario. In the photo, Gregordio was standing with support of a walker.

During the rest of my time in Honduras, Mario showed me around the country I had fallen in love with over and over again through its people. Mario then invited me to visit an orphanage for boys where he used to work. Before driving to the orphanage, we went to a local mall to buy some soccer balls to give to the boys. At the mall's entrance, I noticed a large display case filled with beautiful handmade jewelry. Looking at the beaded bracelets, I was reminded of the open-air markets from past mission trips and how hard the women worked crafting similar bracelets so that they could feed their families. When we arrived at the orphanage, it was clear from their excitement at seeing Mario that the boys knew and loved him. The boys were also grateful for their new soccer balls and invited me to play a game. Before we left, one boy wanted to speak with Mario alone. I could see the boy was upset as he hugged Mario. After we left, I asked Mario what had happened between him and the little boy. Mario explained that many of the boys in orphanages had parents, but the boys were in the orphanage because their parents could not afford to care for them. Many of the boys would run away to look for their families. My heart was breaking not only for the boys, but also for their parents, who had to make such a difficult decision. I am so thankful for Mario for partnering and serving with me again.

"Do not forget to show hospitality to strangers, for by so doing some have shown hospitality to angels without knowing it."
Hebrews 13:2

19

He Goes Before Us
Holy Spirit Fire

Through all of these mission trips, healing miracles, and beautiful, loving people, I learned never to take anything for granted when serving God and serving others. No one can ever out gift God! I learned that God blesses anyone He chooses to bless with gifts, and often His spirit will move in places one might least expect. He truly is the same today as He was yesterday.

While I wait to be called to my next mission trip, Jesus has called me to continue to lay hands over people struggling with pain and health issues in hospitals, homes, or wherever I am. The feeling of heat in my hands seems to be a common factor in each healing, although the sense of movement or vibration varies. I have heard others say the healing heat that I experience is often referred to as fire from the Holy Spirit. The Holy Spirit will not only be around you but placed in your heart and mind by God if you are a follower of Jesus.

As I continue to grow closer to God and use the Holy Spirit's gifts, I know I will be led to many different people in different places, and I will always remain open to doing whatever God calls me to do.

"Truly I tell you, whatever you did for the least of these
brothers and sisters of mine,
you did for me."
Matthew 25:40

"For the kingdom of God is not a matter of eating and
drinking, but of righteousness, peace,
and joy in the Holy Spirit."

Romans 14:17

Acknowledgment

My husband for many years of love and support
My sons and grandchildren who continue to fill my life
with joy
My Mother and sisters who have become my forever
friends
My church family and selfless prayer warriors who have
served alongside me
My Grandma Carr and Dad whose love I will carry in my
heart forever
All those who have been a part of my journey, you have
blessed my life richly.

Made in the USA
Middletown, DE
13 June 2021